KNOTS

USEFUL AND ORNAMENTAL

KNOTS

USEFUL AND ORNAMENTAL

BY

GEORGE RUSSELL SHAW

BONANZA BOOKS · NEW YORK

Printed In the United States

ISBN: 517K01453

This edition published by Bonanza Books,
a division of Crown Publishers, Inc.,
by arrangement with Houghton Mifflin Company
f g h

INSCRIBED
TO
ROBERT GOULD SHAW
BY HIS
BROTHER

N the United States, the study of knots has moved westward and may be found in the curriculum of western State Colleges. There the AB seaman, the familiar tar of the deep seas, finds a worthy coadjutor in the Mexican Vaquerro, the mounted Cowboy, skilful in the training of horses, in the embellishment of saddlery, very skilful with the rope, bringing with him names of Spanish origin — lasso, cinch, lariat, latigo hondo — now permanently grafted on the English tongue as it is spoken in all the ranches beyond the Mississippi.

In many details incidental to the care and breeding of stock, to the cultivation of land, to the harvest, its storage and transportation, there are occasions for the use of cordage where the knowledge of reliable knots, appropriate for whatso ever emergency, is an important part of the ranchmans education.

In the first edition, #64 braid of the New Bedford Textile Co. was recommended for practice in tying knots. If the ends when cut, are dipped in paste or rubber cement and are rolled between the fingers, the strands will not unravel and a rigid end will result, very convenient for reeving through eyelets or loops.

CONTENTS

CONTENTS

1
DEFINITIONS

The <u>End</u> of a Line
   is the part that ties the Knot
   shown thus
           on the drawings

The Standing Part
   is the rest of the Line
   shown unfinished
           on the drawings
              as at A

   A

   Standing Part

End

<u>The</u> Bight is the part of the line between its ends

<u>A Bight</u>
   is a more or less pronounced
              bend
   in a line – Figs. II, a or b

II-a

II-b

A knot may be tied
   with the End
      Fig. III
        or
   with the Bight
      Fig. IV

III

IV

2

A HITCH
as here understood
is a Knot
tied to a
ring, spar, post, cable
or
other anchorage
not a part of the knot itself

Figs. I, II, III.

A BEND
is a Knot uniting
two lines
or two parts of the same line
where
each line or each part
is an integral part of the Knot

Figs IV, V, VI.

3
NOOSE and LOOP

A Noose
is tied with
a Hitch
of one of its parts A·A
around the other B~B,
which remains straight. Fig. 1

A Loop
is tied with
a Bend
where both parts C & D combine
to form the Knot
Fig II

A Noose Fig. 1
may become a Loop Fig III
by tying a Hitch
in the
running part B

A Loop Fig II
may become a Noose Fig IV
when one
of its parts C-C-C
can be straightened

4

HALF HITCH

A round turn of a line about
a post or a spar
One part
of the line
bears or jams upon the other
Figs. I & II

or

A turn
of the end of a line
around the
standing part
Figs III, IV

In Fig. V by
pulling B down
and A up
the hitch M
will be
transferred to
the other
part of the line
Fig. VI

M
V   VI
M

B   B

A   A

In Fig. VI
by
pulling A down
and B up
the hitch M
regains
its original
position

5
TWO
HALF HITCHES

It will be seen later
that the knot
of
Fig.I - Lark
is a form of the
Reef Knot
page
19
Fig II - Clove
is a form of the
Granny

Page 32

I
Lark

II
Clove

Fig. III - Crossed Lark is
a form of the
Oblique Square Knot
page 20

Fig IV - Crossed Clove, of
the
Oblique Granny
page 33

III
Crossed
Lark

IV
Crossed
Clove

LARK'S HEAD

II

I

III

IV - a

Double
Lark's Head

IV - b

V - a

V - b

Triple Lark's Head
Figs. V-a & V-b

7
CLOVE HITCH

Two Half Hitches of the
same lay
over
a post

over the finger

8
CLOVE HITCH

with
Double Loop
Figs. I—III

I

II

III

Clove Hitch
and
Overhand
Knot

IV

V

VI

a   b   c

See
page 94

Magnus Hitch

OVERHAND KNOT

Figs. I, II
Overhand Knot

Fig. III
Overhand Noose
The knot tied with the bight of the line

Overhand Bend

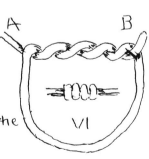

Multiple
Overhand Knots
Pull A & B sharply
Figs. V, VI
Fig. V is also known as the
Blood Knot

10
TWIN
OVERHAND KNOTS

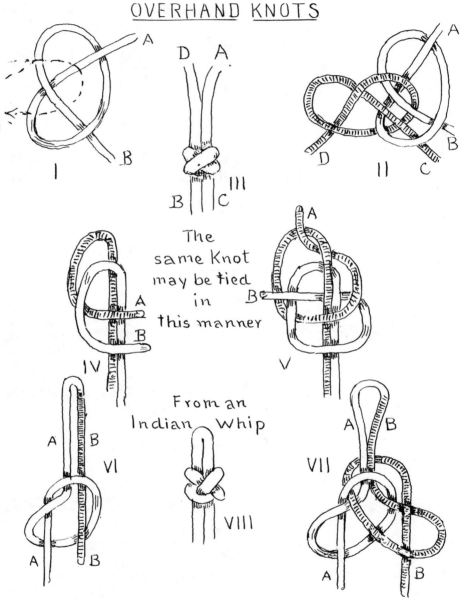

I

D A

B C III

II D C

The
same Knot
may be tied
in
this manner

IV

A
B

V

B

From an
Indian Whip

VI

A B

A B

VIII

VII

A B

A B

11

THE OVERHAND
KNOT

when tied with a paper
band
takes the form of
a pentagon

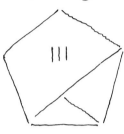

Let one end
of a length of tape
be turned over
three times
and then be pasted
onto the
other end, Fig. IV

If the tape is
cut through along
the dotted line
it becomes an endless
Overhand Knot
Fig. V.

12
FIGURE OF EIGHT

FIGURE OF EIGHT BEND

Figure of Eight and the
Miller's Knot

See page 106

Fig. of 8

Lay A over
onto B
Figs. 1, 11

Miller's Knot

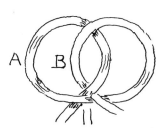

Throw the two loops
over a post
Fig III

The Overhand Knot
Fig. IV
can also pass
into the
Miller's Knot
by shifting C & D

13
FIGURE of EIGHT

Packer's Noose

Stevedore Knot

Single Figure of Eight

III   IV   V

Double Figure of Eight
Figs. VI–VIII

VI   VIII   VII

Multiple Figure of Eight
Figs. IX, X

IX   B   A

X   A   B

ANALYSIS
of the Bends of the
forms M & N

___

CENTER

A One line lies on the other

B The two lines interlace

ENDS

Ends
not crossed in
the Bight

1 – Ends on same side
of the Bight

2 – Ends on different
sides of Bight

Ends
are crossed in
the Bight

3 – The Braiding is not
regular

4 – The Braiding is
regular

There are 20 possible combinations

1-A-1 1-A-2 1-A-3 1-A-4 2-A-2 2-A-3 2-A-4 3-A-3 3-A-4 4-A-4
1-B-1 1-B-2 1-B-3 1-B-4 2-B-2 2-B-3 2-B-4 3-B-3 3-B-4 4-B-4

15

Among the twenty
combinations
there are eight knots

REEF KNOT

WEAVER'S KNOT

HALF GRANNY

GRANNY

SINGLE CARRICK

HALF CARRICK

DOUBLE CARRICK (1)

DOUBLE CARRICK (2)

SQUARE KNOT

16

WEAVER'S KNOT

A · C · I · B · C · D

C · II · B · A · D

Beginning with the
Square Knot
Fig. I

HALF GRANNY

GRANNY

C · III · D · A · B

A · IV · D · C · B

See page 30

and ending with the
Double Carrick
Fig. VIII

SINGLE CARRICK

DOUBLE CARRICK

A · V · B · C · C · D

C · 1 · VI · B · A · D

the eight Bends of the previous page
pass, each into the next,
by a slight change
in the
lay of the
strands

HALF CARRICK

DOUBLE CARRICK
-2-

C · VII · D · A · B

VIII

OBLIQUE BENDS

The strands
of the eight bends
are drawn
together
by pulling the ends
A and D
or
B and C

the strain
being directly
parallel
with the axis
M-N

But the strain can be applied to <u>A and C</u> or to <u>B and D</u>
in a direction oblique to the axis.
The Oblique Bends will be explained in later pages
where each is an intermediate stage
in the tying of a Loop peculiar to that Bend alone

The distinction between Direct and Oblique is better
presented when the Bends are tied with the ends of
a single line

The two ends
A & B are on the same
side of the knot

The two ends
B & D are on opposite sides
of the Knot

SQUARE KNOT or REEF KNOT

Tie an Overhand Knot

in such manner that the parts A A lie on the same side of the bight C
Fig. III

Tie another backwards
Fig. II

Fig. IV is the Single Bow Knot tied with the bight of one end

Fig V is the Double Bow Knot tied with the bight of both ends

SQUARE KNOT AND LARK'S HEAD

Fig. 1
is a Loop tied with
a
Square Knot.

If the part A B
is
straightened
the knot becomes
a Noose
tied by a Lark's Head CD
around
the part A-B, Fig. 11

Conversely
A
Lark's Head
around
a line AB, Fig III
becomes a Square Knot by
turning the bight M
around AB
& bringing the ends A&B
together

See page 5, Fig I

To untie a Square Knot, straighten one of the 2 strands
Grasp the resulting Lark's Head·
and strip it quickly from the straight strand

20

OBLIQUE SQUARE KNOT

I

In Fig II pass A to left under, and B to right over the strands

II

A

B

M

The Oblique square knot also known as the Thief Knot

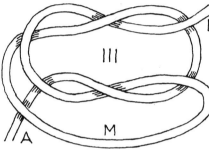

III

B

A

M

Under strain, however slight, it slips apart.

IV

M

A B

See page 5

_____

But in Fig. III bring the ends A & B together, Fig IV. then with A & B in one hand and the part M in the other hand the knot becomes a reliable Japanese Loop.

V

M

See page 148

21
MARLINE -
OR ROPE YARN KNOT

Marline is laid with two strands

The Surgeons' Knot is a
Square Knot
of which
th first part, Fig. V-a,
is a
double Overhand Knot

The Shoe String Knot
A Bow Knot
of which
the
second part
is a
double
Overhand
Knot

Under several names as
Weaver's Knot – Sheet Bend – Bowline & others, is
a combination of a Loop AB with
a Half Hitch CD

Fig. I
is the Direct form of the knot,
the two ends (both A and C)
being on the same side of the knot
Fig. II
is the Oblique form of the knot.
the two ends A & C being
on opposite sides
Fig. III
is the Oblique form
tied with one line.
Fig. IV
A & C are brought
together.

With
C A in one hand &
M in the other

The Knot
becomes a loop

23
WEAVER'S KNOT

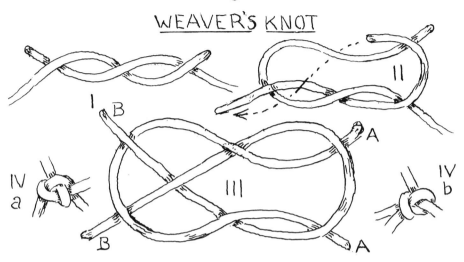

WEAVER'S KNOT
and SLIP NOOSE

Straighten the line A A Fig III
to obtain Fig. V (Crabber's Knot, p 27)

With A A pull bb until the knot
becomes a Noose
Fig. VI

Therefore
the Weaver's Knot may be tied
as follows

Tie a Noose with one line,
pass the other line through its eye
Fig. VI

Hold A A together, pull B and slip
the collar, M, up onto the loop formed by A A, Fig. VII

24
WEAVER'S KNOT

I

II

III

Another Method
Figs. IV, V, VI

IV

V

VI

The combination of a Loop with a Half Hitch
Is a reliable Knot
for joining two lines of
unequal size

HEAVING LINE
BEND

DOUBLE SHEET BEND

WHIP LASH KNOT

BOWLINE

Lay the end A on the standing
part B

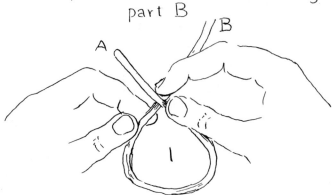

Turn the palm of the right hand up,
forming a loop with the end A through the loop

Pass A around B
and
down through loop.

Figs. III, IV
Obverse and Reverse
of the Knot

RUNNING BOWLINE

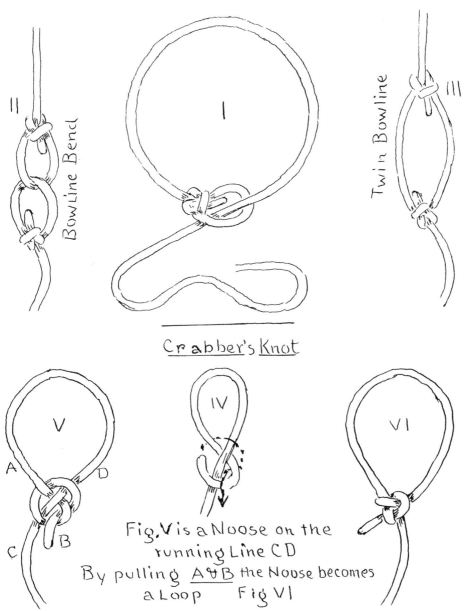

Bowline Bend II

Twin Bowline III

I

Crabber's Knot

V

IV

A   D

C   B

VI

Fig. V is a Noose on the
running Line CD
By pulling A & B the Noose becomes
a Loop   Fig VI

PORTUGUESE BOWLINE

Chaise de Calfat   Caulker's Chair

Fig. I - is a double Loop

Fig. II - where end A crosses the part B
tie a Bowline (III - IV)
around
the two lines

the result
is an adjustable
Double Loop

BOWLINE - ON - BIGHT

This Knot
may be tied with the bight
on any part of the line
A short length of a long rope
may be used without
cutting it

A

I

With the Loop A
tie an Overhand Knot
Fig. I

Pass the Loop A
back under the knot
Fig. II

B

II

A

III - a

obverse

A

III - b

reverse

A

With the strands at B
Fig. II
pull the loop A into the position
shown in Figs. III - (a & b).

HALF GRANNY

B

IV

V

A III

This knot, when pulled taut, is peculiar

Figs. IV, V

The two ends lie side by side

The two faces; both obverse and reverse,

are alike.

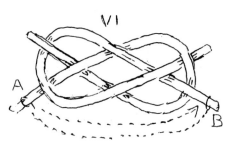

VI

A

B

Fig. VI

is the form of the knot

shown on pages 15-16.

When pulled taut,

it takes the form shown

in Fig. IV (or V)

In Fig. VI interchange A & B

to form VII

In Fig. VII turn the right

hand half of the knot

over to form Fig. VIII

(or Fig. III above)

III, VI & VII, when taut are

alike and are forms of the

HALF GRANNY

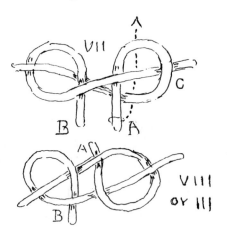

VII

C

B   A

A

VIII

or III

B

THE GRASS KNOT

is the Half Granny as a
bend for straps, straw,
grass or
such flat material

THE REEVING LINE BEND

III

is a form of the Half Granny

NOTE

 IV

 VI

 V

In the Half Granny
Fig. IV
by interchanging
the ends A & B
the knot passes into
the Oblique Granny
Fig. V
The Half Granny must not
be confused with Fig. VI,
which slips and which,
by interchanging
C and D,
passes into the
Thief (Oblique Reef) Knot Fig. VII

THE GRANNY

Tie an
Over hand Knot
Fig I

Tie
another backwards
Fig II

in such manner that
the ends A A
lie on opposite sides of the bight C

GRANNY
and
CLOVE HITCH

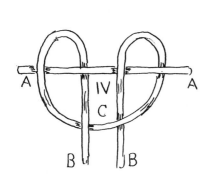

See page 5, Fig II

Straighten
the line A A , Fig III
The parts BB-C become a
Clove Hitch
around the line AA

A Granny, therefore, may be tied as follows.

Tie a
Clove Hitch
around the line
A A
Fig. IV

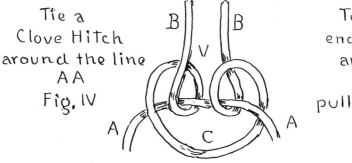

Turn the
ends BB up
around A
and
pull BB and C
Fig.V

OBLIQUE GRANNY

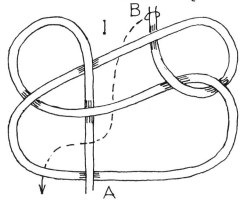

Fig I is the Half Granny.
Pass the end B down
under two strands and
over the strand A.
The knot becomes
Fig II
The Oblique Granny

When this knot
is pulled taut,
it slips apart
and will not
hold.

But, by bringing the ends
A & B together Fig. II,
by holding A & B in one
hand and the part M
in the other, Fig II
becomes a reliable Loop.

See page 5

The Japanese method of tying
this Loop is shown on page 148.

BUNTLINE HITCH AND OBLIQUE GRANNY

Fig. 1
Pull the bight of C
under B
as shown in Fig II

Holding
A & C
in
place

pull D
slowly to
form
Fig III

Buntline
Hitch

The
Oblique Granny

FOUR-IN-HAND TIE

Buntline Hitch

SINGLE CARRICK BEND

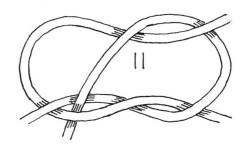

The two bights that form
the finished knot, lie on
planes perpendicular to
each other.
The lay of the strands
resembles that of the
four strand Round Braid.

III

Single Carrick

Fig. IV
Single Carrick
and Fig. V
Half Carrick
are very much alike.
They differ in the
braiding of their
strands,
alternately
over and under
in Fig V
very irregular
in Fig IV

Half Carrick

IV

V

36
DOUBLE CARRICK
No. 1

This Knot
differs from
the Double Carrick No 2
by the
irregular braiding
of the strands

I

II

III

Fig. V begins with an
Overhand Knot Fig. IV

Fig. VII begins with the
Miller's Knot Fig. VI

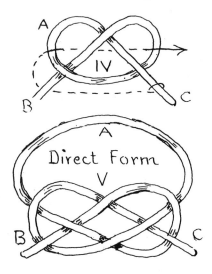

A

IV

B   C

A

Direct Form

V

B   C

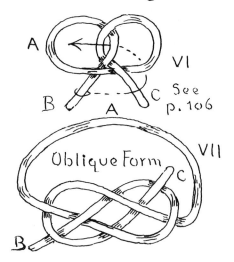

A

VI

B   A   C See
p. 106

Oblique Form

VII

C

B

HALF CARRICK

This is Nameless-2 of the first edition

The strands of the
Half Carrick
in one half (M) of the knot, have the lay characteristic
of the Double Carrick-No.2,
The strands of the other half (N) correspond with the
lay of the Granny.

So far as I know
this knot
is not in use

OBLIQUE HALF CARRICK

In Fig II
bring the ends
A & B
together

Fig III
Hold A & B
in one hand and
pull M

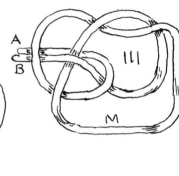

HALF CARRICK and MILLER'S KNOT

Fig. V,
the Miller's Knot
(pages 12, 106)
can pass
by a slight change
into Fig. VI,
the Half Carrick

DOUBLE CARRICK
No. 2

This knot
differs from the
Double Carrick No 1
by the
regular braiding
of its strands

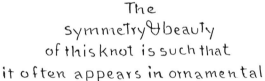

The
symmetry & beauty
of this knot is such that
it often appears in ornamental
combinations

See pages
143, 147, 188 &c.

40

OBLIQUE DOUBLE CARRICK
No. 2

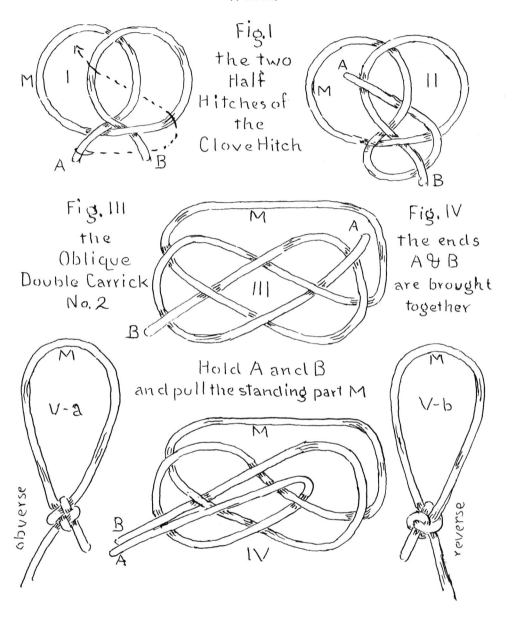

Fig. I
the two
Half
Hitches of
the
Clove Hitch

Fig. III
the
Oblique
Double Carrick
No. 2

Fig. IV
the ends
A & B
are brought
together

Hold A and B
and pull the standing part M

obverse

V-a

reverse

V-b

41

NOOSE

Halter
Tie
Figs. I, II, III

Figure of 8
Tie
Figs. IV, V, VI
See page 103

I

IV

Overhand Noose

II

III

V

VI

DOUBLE NOOSE

I

C

B

C

A

II

A

C

B

C

III

C

B

C

A

A

C

IV

B

HANGMAN'S NOOSE

pull

The Hangman's Noose is tied with eight or nine turns of the rope

LOOP

Noose & Half Hitch

The size of the loop
may be changed
after the knot is tied
→ by manipulating XY

I

II

Japanese Loops

see pages 20 148

see pages 40 49

see pages 33 148

hold

Angler's Loop
I-IV

I

II

III

IV

pull

44
ARTILLERY
or
MAN – HARNESS
KNOT

The
Knots on pages
Forty four
to
Forty seven

are
tied with
the bight
of
the line

45

LINEMAN'S KNOT

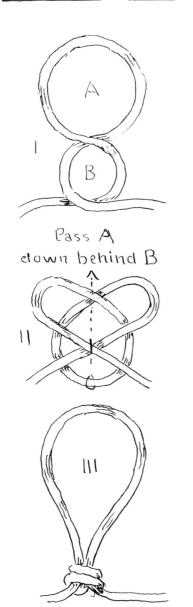

I

Pass A
down behind B

II

III

LOOP

beginning with an
Overhand Knot

Fig. 1

I

Pull

II

Pull

III

DOUBLE LOOP

In Fig. IV,
pull the loop A & the end B
to form Fig. V

DOUBLE LOOPS

Spanish Bowline

In Fig. II
Turn the crotch B
over onto the crotch C

In Fig. IV the strand MN
is a running line

Another
Double Loop

The strand XY   is a running line

STOPPER KNOTS

49
STOPPER KNOT
of two
Strands

Fig II
Pass A under B
to Form
Fig. III - The Oblique Granny

Fig. II is the Half
Granny

I

II

A

B

III

B

A

IV

B

A

VI

V

B

A

50
WALL KNOT

With 3 cords
the Wall may be
tied
to the right
or
to the left

With a
rope
the Wall must
follow
the lay of the
strands

CROWN KNOT

51

MAN-ROPE KNOT

A combination of the Wall & Crown with the strands doubled

I

Single Wall

II

Single Wall & Crown

Top

In doubling each strand follows its own lay

V

The Crown Fig. II brings each end against its own part

III

Double Wall & Single Crown

The 3 ends A B C Fig III are passed down through the center of the knot Fig. IV and are cut off

IV

Double Wall & Crown

52

TWIN WALL KNOT

Wall A & B together
around C & D
Fig I, II

C & D are
walled together
following the dotted lines

53
DIAMOND KNOT

Fig. II

Pass 1 around the thumb,
2 around the forefinger,
3 around the little finger
forming 3 loops

Fig. III

Pass the ends through the loops
in the order shown

or

54
DIAMOND KNOT
of
Four
Strands

III

II

DIAMOND
of
Two Strands

Fig IV
The
Oblique
Double Carrick
No 2
See page 40
Fig III

IV

VII

V

VI

55
DOUBLE DIAMOND

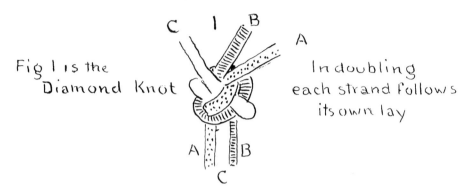

Fig I is the
Diamond Knot

In doubling
each strand follows
its own lay

For practise with this, and with the various
Stopper Knots.
the construction is more easily followed if the strands
are of different colors.

First stage.
In Fig. 1
{ pass A over C & under B
pass B over A & under C
pass C over B & under A
to form Fig II

Second stage
In Fig. II
{ pass A over both strands of C & under both strands of B
pass B over both strands of A & under both strands of C
pass C over both strands of B & under both strands of A

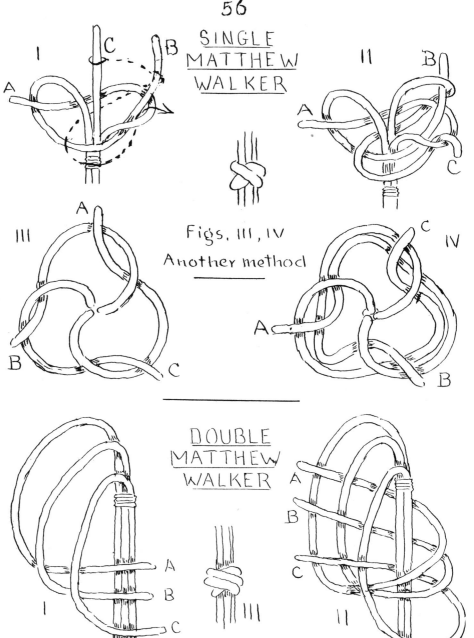

56

SINGLE MATTHEW WALKER

Figs. III, IV
Another method

DOUBLE MATTHEW WALKER

INVERTED WALL KNOT

<u>Button of 3 Strands</u>

II   C   B   A

I   C   A   B

III   B   C   A

In Fig III
the 3 strands
A, B & C
are
crowned

In Fig. IV
the 3 ends are passed down
through the centre and cutt off

IV

<u>Button of
4 strands</u>

V   VI

VII   VIII

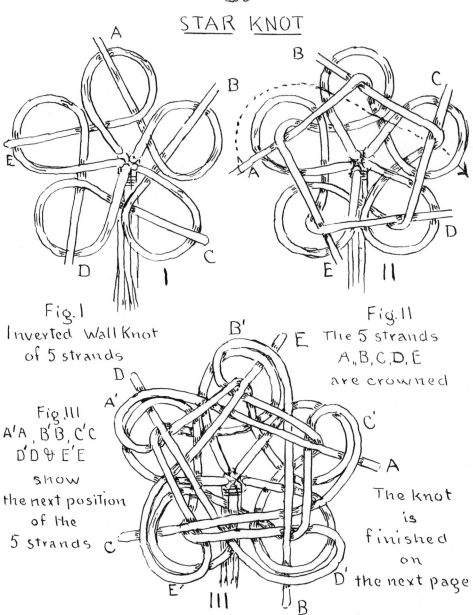

58

STAR KNOT

Fig. I
Inverted Wall Knot
of 5 strands

Fig. II
The 5 strands
A, B, C, D, E
are crowned

Fig. III
A'A, B'B, C'C
D'D & E'E
show
the next position
of the
5 strands

The knot
is
finished
on
the next page

59

STAR KNOT
Continued

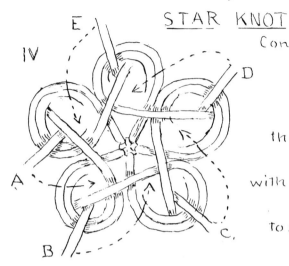

IV

E

D

A

B

C

Fig IV

is

the reverse side of

Fig. III

with some of the strands

omitted

to avoid confusion

Fig V

(reverse side)

The ends A, B, C, D and E
following the arrows in Fig IV
pass up through
the bights and the center of the

knot

V

VI

VIII

TURK'S HEAD

A Turk's Head may be defined
as a complex of like interlacing circles
so united as to form a single line, and whose centers are
the angles of a regular polygon of 3, 4, 5 or of any conve-
-nient number of sides.

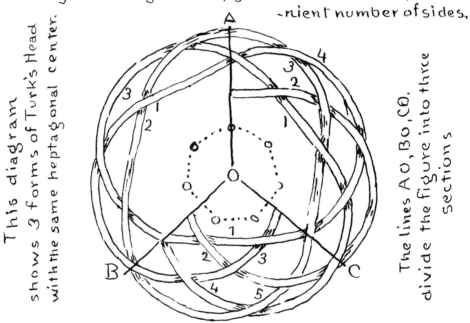

This diagram shows 3 forms of Turk's Head with the same heptagonal center.

The lines AO, BO, CO divide the figure into three sections.

The section AOB
represents a heptagonal Turk's Head of three strands

the section AOC | the section BOC
of 4 strands | of 5 strands

TURK'S HEAD
Triangular Center
Two strands

This Turk's Head
is the
Overhand Knot
Fig. IV

A Triangular Turk's Head
with 4 strands

In this Turk's Head the circles
are joined in one line
by means of
loops
a, b, c.

On account of the crowded
interlacing
at the center of the knot
this method is not practicable
for centers of four or more sides

TURK'S HEAD

Quadrangular Center

Three strands

This Turk's Head is the

Double Carrick Bend, No. 2

Fig 1

63
TURK'S HEAD

of
3 strands
and
pentangular center

A   B

B   A

Fig. I
is
a form of
the
Figure of Eight
Knot
page 12

A

B ||| 3
2   1

I

II

Turn III half over to show Fig. IV

III

IV   V   VI   VII

TURK'S HEAD

pentagonal,
of
three strands,
tied on the
hand

I
palm

II
Back

V
palm

III
Back

IV
palm

Fig IV — The bights are crossed
at A

65
TURK'S HEAD
of
four strands
and pentangular center

I

Fig1
is the
Overhand
Knot

III

II

V

VI

IV

I

II

IV

III

66
TURK'S HEAD
as a
Stopper
Knot

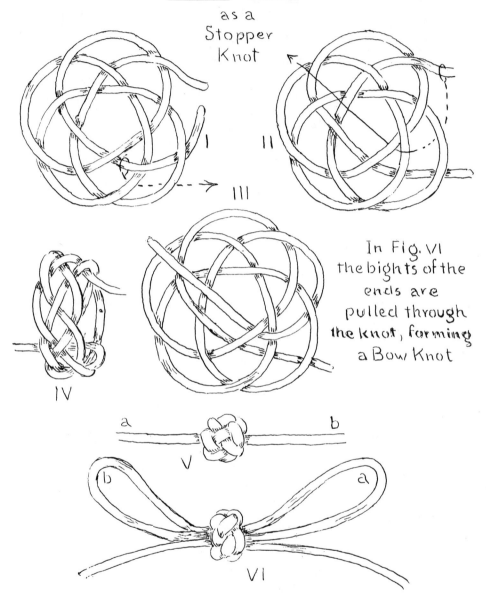

I

II

III

IV

In Fig. VI
the bights of the
ends are
pulled through
the knot, forming
a Bow Knot

a   b

V

b   a

VI

67
TURK'S HEAD
as a
BUTTON

Fig.1- Turk's Head

Fig.II-The strands
are double

Fig.III
End A carried down through
the Knot

Fig.IV
End B is carried down
and back through
the Knot
Forming two loops
B' and B"

top of knot

Fig.V
A and B' are crowned
and are passed up through
the centre of the crown
coming out
alongside of B-B"
All ends are cut off except
one loop
Fig.VI

68

SENNIT

Plaiting with an uneven number of strands

The outer strands in alternate order pass over 2 strands, Fig 1, 3 strands, Fig 2, (or any convenient number) meeting in a "herring-bone" central line

---

FRENCH SENNIT

The strands in this method may be odd or even in number

69
SENNIT

Of Five Strands

Of Seven Strands

Of Nine Strands

SENNIT
of three Strands
Forming
a
Ring

The Ring
may be tied
around 4, 6, 8,
or
any even number of
pins

Fig. I
Begin at A.
Carry the line A B
around outside of pins
Thereafter the line lies
alternately outside and
inside of the pins - Fig. II, III

Fig. IV
The strands of
Fig III
are thrown over
a post,
The strands
may be
doubled
or
tripled

Fig. V
is the same Sennit
tied around six pins.

SENNIT

of Five and Seven Strands forming Rings
In addition to the four fixed pins, others are needed to
hold the work
in place

Figs. I-II-III
Five-strand
Sennit

Figs. I-IV-V
Seven-Strand
Sennit

THREE-STRAND SENNITS

tied with one line

Overhand Knot

Figure of Eight Knot

TRIANGULAR BRAID OF TWO STRANDS

Fig. I   A loop C is formed
by tying an Overhand
Knot with the bight
of strand A

Fig II _ With the fingers
through the loop C
seize B, pull it through
the loop C,
at the
same time
pull A
thus forming
a
new Loop D

Fig. IV
With the fingers through D
form a new Loop with the bight of A, and by pulling B,
and so on, forming loops
alternately
with the two strands

The three faces of
the Braid

SINGLE STRAND SQUARE BRAID

Fig I
Arrangement
of the cord A B
on the fork

Fig II
Pass the Slipnoose C
over E & N

Fig III
Draw C taut with A
(A is no longer used). N

The braid begins
Fig IV
Pass B around M
at F
Fig V
Pass D over F & M

Pull D taut First with 1 — next with 2 — Then with B

Fig VI
Pass B around N
at G
Pass E over G & N
Tighten with 3 pulls
and so on

75

BRAID
OF THREE STRANDS

Three strands
A, B, C

B & C forming
Nooses
D E

Much
enlarged

A

M

N

F

G

D

E

B

C

I

II

A is passed
around
the prong M
at F

B is passed
around
the prong N
at G

The loop D is passed
over F & M
and is drawn taut
with B

The loop E is passed
over G and N
and is pulled taut
with C

III

C is then passed around M etc.
The strand that pulls its loop taut forms the next
new loop
The arrows at F & G indicate the lay of the
strands that form the new loops.

FOUR-STRAND ROUND BRAID

A B C D

The strands A&B
are always the left hand,
the strands C&D
are always the right hand, couple

I

B A C D

II

B A D C

III

The Braid can be tied
when 2 of the strands form a loop
Figs. IV–VI

IV

VI

V

77

ROUND BRAID

tied with a doubled strand

With leather straps

FOUR-STRAND FLAT BRAID

I   III   II

Joining two Strands
A and B

Figs. IV, V
the
Carrick Bend B

The Braid can be extended indefinitely at each
end or at both ends   Figs. VI, VII, VIII

Pull
the bights
of
Fig. V

To form
the
Fig. VI

A SIX-STRAND AND EIGHT-STRAND BRAID

Half Round
Braid

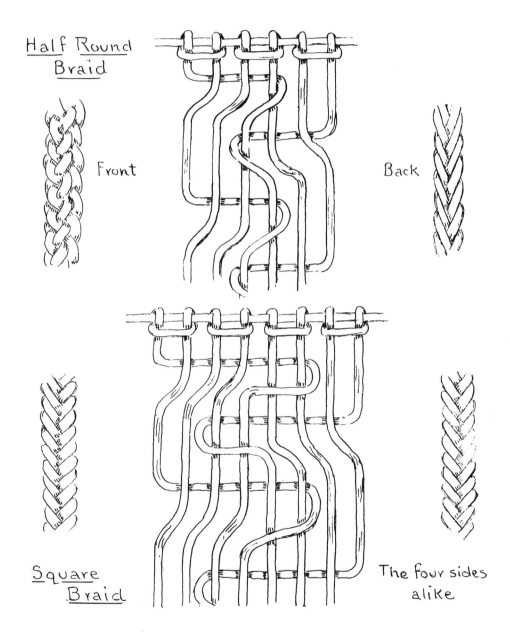

Front

Back

Square
Braid

The four sides
alike

SQUARE BRAID

of ten strands

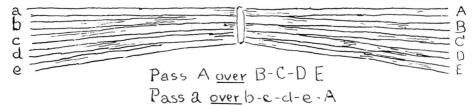

a b c d e ... A B C D E

Pass A _over_ B-C-D E

Pass a _over_ b-c-d-e-A

Pass b _under_ c-d-e-A   Pass B _under_ C-D-E-a-b

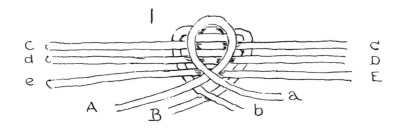

I

c d e ... c D E

A   B   b   a

Pass C _over_ D-E-a-b   Pass c _over_ d-e-A-B-C

Pass d _under_ e-A-B-C   Pass D _under_ E-a-b-c-d

II

e A B C ... E a b c D d

Fig. II repeats the method of Fig. I
and its repetition forms the Braid.

CROWN BRAID

This is the Crown Knot
repeated in superposed layers

Top

Bottom

Figs. VIII, IX
show
the two methods
of tying the
Braid

In Fig. VIII
each strand is laid to & fro
upon itself
reversing, in the alternate layers, the order of rotation

In Fig. IX
the order of rotation is always the same

CROWN BRAID

Fig. I

is the Braid tied by the method of
Fig. VIII on the last page

Fig. II

is the Braid tied by the method of
Fig. IX, on the last page

Six-Strand Braid

_____ III

The Braid may be tied around
a Core, Fig. IV

X

The Core may be pulled out
Fig. V
and, with a copper wire X-Y,
the strands
at each end of the Braid
can be drawn
through the centre, Fig. VI, so as
to form
a neat finish at both ends

CHAIN BRAID

Single   Double

tied with the   tied with the
Bight   End
A   B

The
single
Chain Braid
is the fundamental Knot
in Crochet & Knitting

84
FALSE BRAID
in
Leather

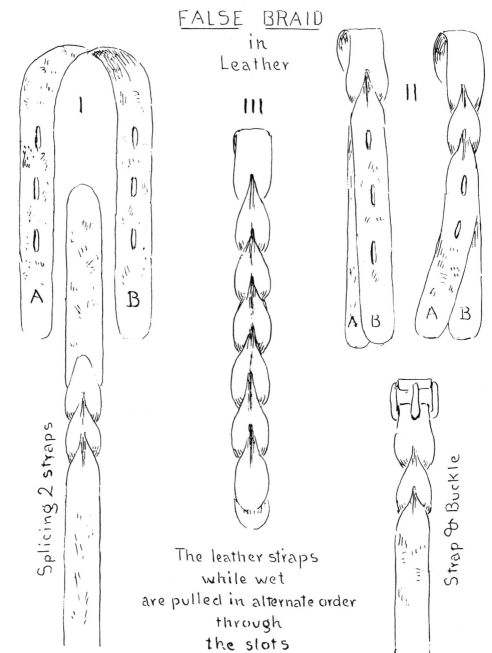

I

III

II

A   B

A   B

Splicing 2 straps

The leather straps
while wet
are pulled in alternate order
through
the slots

Strap & Buckle

85
FALSE BRAID

Three straps may unite in a False Braid
as shown in Fig I

I

Four straps may also be combined as
shown in Fig II

II

The slits are cut one by one as the work progresses

The Braid will be square in cross section
when, with 2 straps, the width of the strap is twice
its thickness—with 3 straps, 3 times, & with
4 straps, 4 times the thickness.

The 3 methods may combine to form a Leash or Quirt

III

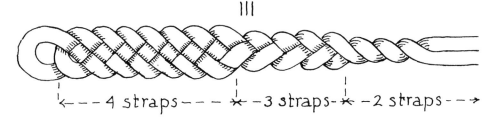

$\longleftarrow$ - - 4 straps - - - $\ast$ - 3 straps - $\ast$ - 2 straps - - $\rightarrow$

86

TRICK BRAID

Fig. I – Leather strap with two slits and three strands

Fig. II – A over B and C over A

Pass M through X

to form Fig. III

Fig IV

B over C, A over B

M through Y.

Repeat

as desired

VI

SAILORS KNOTS
REEVING
LINE

Fig. II is the Half Granny — see page 30

Temporary Bend

Spanish Hawser Bend

VII   VIII

...A...

The Knot at A is the Single Carrick

Figs. IV and V Hawser Bend

HITCHES

Hook and Half Hitch

I

II

III

Figs. I, II
Blackwall

Slippery
Hitch

Drawing Knot
Bowline and Half Hitch

Backhanded Hitch

I - - - - II

HITCHES

Fisherman

Tops'l
Halyard

Rolling
Hitch

Lark's Head & Half Hitch

Midshipman

Chain Hitch

Twists

Timber Hitch

Killick Hitch

Double Twist

CATSPAW

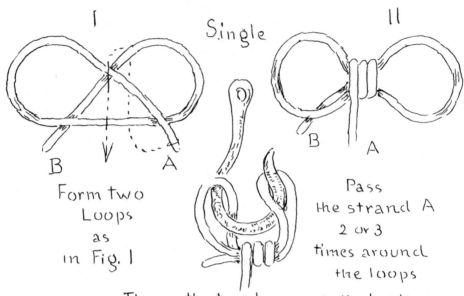

Single

I

B   A

Form two
Loops
as
in Fig. I

II

B   A

Pass
the strand A
2 or 3
times around
the loops

Throw the two loops onto the hook

———

Double

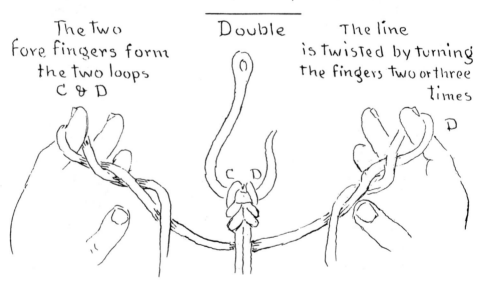

The two
Fore fingers form
the two loops
C & D

The line
is twisted by turning
the fingers two or three
times

91

HEAVING LINE

Figs. I, II
Terminal Knot
of the
Heaving Line

I

II

III

IV

Figs III, IV
Bends
of the Heaving Line and
Hawser

THE TOGGLE

Figs, I,II,III
Strop
Toggle

I

III

Toggle & Lark

IV

V

II

Fig. VI
Sheet Bend
Toggle

VII

Eye Toggle

VI

VIII

Toggle and Sheepshank

IX

MOORING

Over a Post

Tie an Overhand Knot on
the post
with the bight of the
line
and throw the
loop A over the post

Through a Ring

In Fig I
pass the bight of S through
the loop E and pull
the end E

In Fig II
pass bight of E through
the loop S
and pull the end S

The knot is released
by pulling the end E
of III

MOORING

Figs I, II
Two
Half Hitches

Lark's Head

With
bight & toggle

Magnus Hitch

or
as shown on
page 8 — Figure VI

95

WHIPPING

Serving

SPLICING

M   N

Unlay 7 or 8 strands of the two ropes
M and N to be spliced   Arrange them in
such manner that each strand of M lies between
two strands of N and each of N lies between two
strands of M.

Push the six strands close together
and bind them temporarily with twine

SHORT SPLICE   Braiding

Each strand passes over the next one
and then under the second beyond.

SHORT SPLICE

Twisting
the Strands

Twist Together
C & M, A & N, B & O

giving each end
3 or 4 turns

LONG SPLICE

Marry the strands as shown above

Unlay C to X
and replace it with M
& similarly
unlay O to Y
and replace it with B

Tie M & C together with an Overhand Knot
similarly tie together A & N and B & O
Taper the ends
and weave them into the strands of the rope

98

SELVAGEE

Lifting
Hitch

GROMMET

Carefully unlay a single strand of rope twelve times the diameter of the Grommet

Relay the Strand on itself

To Finish split the ends & tie one half of the ends in an Overhand Knot Fig. IV

Split the ends again and tuck them into the strands.

Stretch the finished Grommet and cut away the ends

100

SHEEP SHANK

With both of the ends fast

or

___

With the ends free

Overhand Knot

Fig. of 8

or

KNOTS
OF THE RANCH AND FARM

LASSO

THE HONDA or Hondo
An Eyelet tied with two Overhand Knots

Lasso

HALTERS

Loop with a
<u>Honda</u>
of two
Figure-of-8 knots

I
Honda
open

II
Honda
closed

A   B   A   A

III

Fig. III
<u>Double Noose</u>

C

C

A A, the larger Noose,
is placed
around the neck

B, the smaller Noose,
is placed
over the muzzle

B

HALTER and MANGER
KNOTS

Figure-of-Eight Noose

See page 41

HACKAMORE TIE

This is the
Buntline Hitch
which, by manipulation
of the parts A & B,
may be tied
as a Noose, Fig. IV
or
as a Loop, Fig. V

see page
34

104

HALTER

Bowline

I

II

III

IV

V

SACK KNOTS

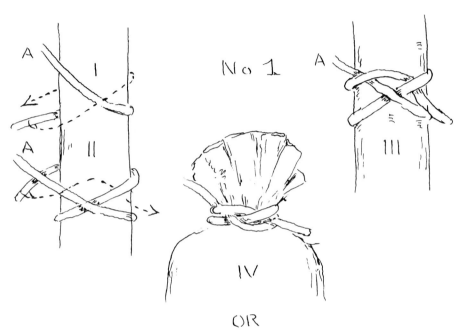

No 1

A   I

A   II

A   III

IV

OR

Tie an Overhand Knot
Fig. V

X

A   V   B

Y

A   B

X   VI

Turn A over
laying X onto Y
Fig. VI

D   D

VII

Lay
A under B
and slip
the two loops
onto D

SACK KNOTS

No. 2

Millers Knot

See
page 12

I

II

III

IV

O R
Tie a Figure of 8 Knot
Fig. V

V

VI

B   A

C

Lay the loop A
onto B
to
form the
Fig VI

Slide
the loop C
onto D

D   D

VII

SACK KNOTS

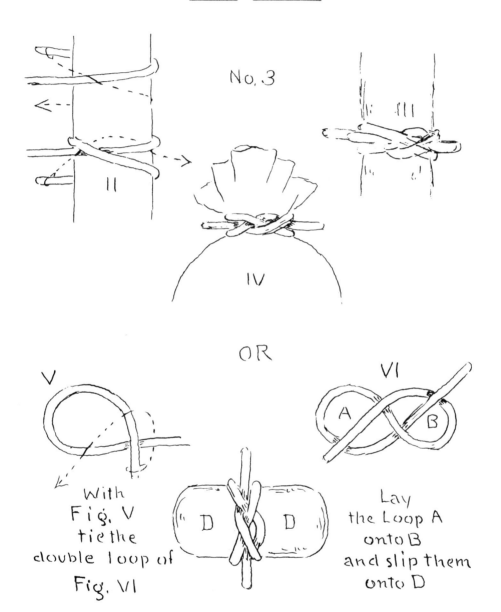

No. 3

II

III

IV

OR

V

VI

A   B

With
Fig. V
tie the
double loop of
Fig. VI

D   D

Lay
the Loop A
onto B
and slip them
onto D

SACK KNOTS

N̄o. 4

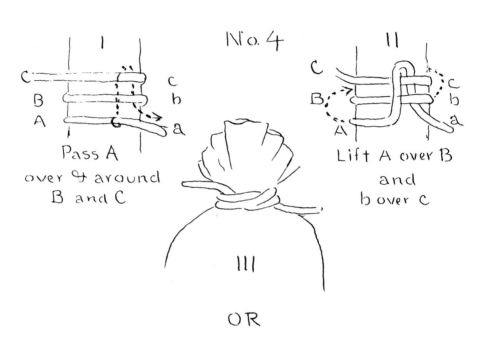

I

C ——
B
A

c
b
a

Pass A
over & around
B and C

II

C
B
A

c
b
a

Lift A over B
and
b over c

III

OR

Tie a Blood Knot
Fig. IV

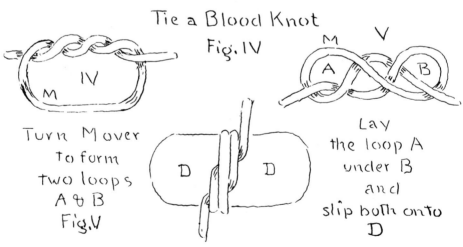

IV

M

Turn M over
to form
two loops
A & B
Fig. V

V

M

A

B

Lay
the loop A
under B
and
slip both onto
D

D   D

DIAMOND HITCH

A compensating device for
secoring the pack
on a horse

The rope is adjusted to form
a quadrangle
on the top of the pack.

The strain that tends to pull A & B apart
is held in check
by a counter-strain at
the points
C & D

JAR SLING

In Fig.III
pass the loop A down
to the position
shown in
Fig.IV

In Fig IV
pass the loop B
down to
the position of B
in
Fig.V

SLINGS

111

Can

Fig. 1
Tie an Overhand Knot vertically around the can

Spread the knot apart and fit it around the top of the can A-Fig.III
Tie the ends together_B, Fig III

Arrange the rope as in Fig. IV

Set the barrel on the rope Fig.V

Barrel

112

<u>LADDERS</u>

- - - - Single-rope Ladder - - -

Oak Chock

The Chocks are stopped by a 4-strand Diamond – Fig.11

Pass 2 lines A-B, C-D through the Rope

All-rope Ladder

113
ANGLER'S KNOTS
Line and Leader

Line

Line

Line

Leader

Leader

Leader

Hook and Leader

TYING LEADERS

Barrel Knot

I

Water Knot

II

Water Loop

III

May be tied as in Figs. III, IV, VII,
or as in Figs. V, VI, VII

IV

VII

V

VI

For Angler's Loop see page 43

115

TYING FLIES

A simple and effective
artificial fly
may be tied with a fish hook,
a length of colored silk,
and a hackle from the neck of a cock.

II

Tying on the hackle

III

Winding the
waxed silk

IV

Fig. V
A few close turns
of the hackle

Fig VI
The silk
secures the
butt of the hackle
and is whipped on to
the hook

V

VI

to form the head of the fly — A drop of varnish on the head

116
FISHERMAN'S NET

The Knot
is the same as
the Sheet Bend, Bowline &c.
It is a Half Hitch
combined
with
a Loop

Fig.I - the Loop

Fig.II   Loop and
   Half Hitch

Fig III
    A B C
   represents the
      Loop

Fig IV
   The end D
      ties
   the Half Hitch

Shuttle

V

Mesh

III

A

C

B

D

A

D

IV

B

C

D

D

117

CIRCULAR NET

Fig. I
Tie 6 loops
on a centre loop

Fig II
Tie 2 Knots on each loop

I

II

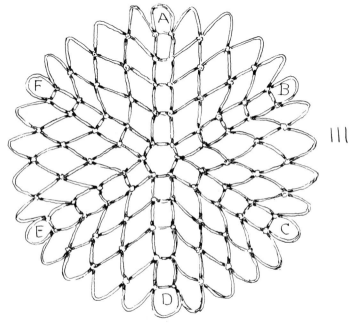

III

Fig III
The diameter of the net
increases
by tying 2 Knots
on each of the loops that lie on
the three lines
AD-BE-CF

TENNIS NET

This net can be tied

without mesh or shuttle

Tied with short lines – A, A

A   A   A   A

The net should be hung on a wire rope which is fixed permanently in position

The net and its Fringe should be 2 ft. 6 in. deep and, when hung, 6 in. above the ground

119
NETTING

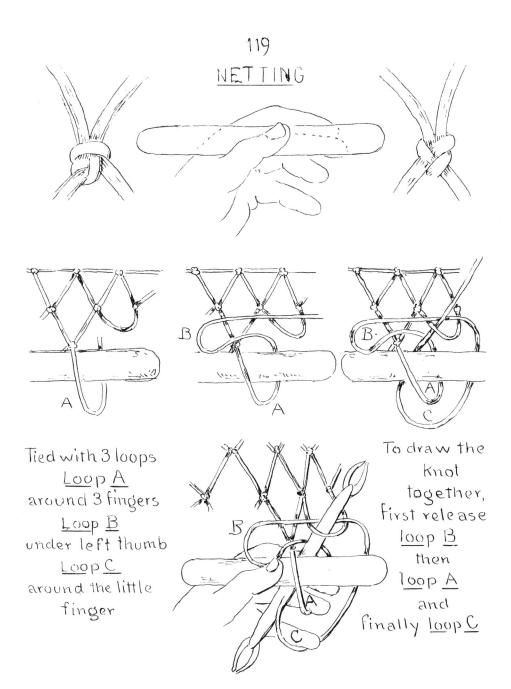

Tied with 3 loops
Loop A
around 3 fingers
Loop B
under left thumb
Loop C
around the little
finger

To draw the
knot
together,
first release
loop B
then
loop A
and
finally loop C

120

TYING

PACKAGES

Front

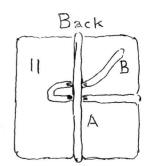

Back

Fig. I
Begin with the Packers' Noose

Back

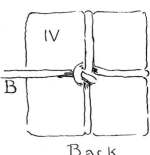

Back

Fig II
Pass the bight of the line under the strand A

Fig. III
With the bight draw the strand A taut

Fig. IV
Pass the end B through the bight and draw the knot taut

Figs. V and VI
Finish with two or three Half Hitches

Front

Front

TYING
PACKAGES

Fig 1
Introduced here as a not-too-difficult puzzle
{ To tie a 4-strand package
with a single line, the beginning and the end not shown }

Diamond Tie

122

JAPANESE

KNOTS

123
KNIFE — LANYARD

124
WATCH FOB

Begin with a doubled line
A – Fig. I
Add another doubled line
B – Fig. II

I

II

III

Wall the four strands
together

IV

Begin the Crown Braid
page 81

V

Finish with a
4-strand Double
Diamond

VII

Top

Crown the ends
and pass them down
through the Knot and
cut them off

125

GIRDLE

Begin
with the middle ring
—
There are
from 15 to 25
brass rings
one inch in diameter

A

A

← 1 in. →

Button of wood
or of bone

Detail
at B

Detail
at A

Brass ring

The material is silk braid
one tenth of an inch
in diameter

LEATHER FASTENING
FOR
A Girdle

A

A

A

Girdle

B

B
C

D

E

B

There are 2 loops – A – ⅛ inch wide. The thongs
are doubled at B. The 4 thongs of each loop are braided – C.
At the end of the Braids the 2 loops (A–A) are tied together.
D is a Turk's Head. The 8 thongs are split, forming a
tassel of 16 strands.

LEATHER BELT
and
BUCKLE

Fig. 1
A - Part of Belt
slit into
three Strands _ See page 86

Fig. 1
B - Two iron or
brass rings

A

B

Fig II-A-The strands braided -B- The buckle fastened

A

B

Fig. III - The inside of Buckle _ The rings enlarged
to show method more
clearly

MACRAMÉ KNOTS

These are
The Square Knot, the Half Hitch and the Granny
tied around
one or more idle lines
drawn taut

Square Knot   Half Hitch   Granny

MACRAME KNOTS

TATTING LOOP

Fig. I
A Half Hitch
of the end A
around the end B

Fig. II
By pulling
x & A
B becomes a Half Hitch
around A

Fig III
A ties a second Half Hitch
which is also upset by pulling
x and A
These 2 knots form
a Lark's Head Fig IV

The Tatting Loop
is a row of such Lark's Heads

By
pulling A, Fig VIII
The Lark's Heads
are drawn

upon a
running
line

into
the form
of
a loop IX

131

TATTING

Fig I   Loop

Insertion

Fig. II
Round Braid

See page 77

Lace

Insertion

Fig III
Diamond Knot

Fig. IV
Water Knot

Lace

BOOK COVER

ORIENTAL RUGS

Turkish Knot   Persian Knot

Five hundred knots
to the square inch are not unusual

KNOTS
IN
HERALDRY

CHINESE KNOT

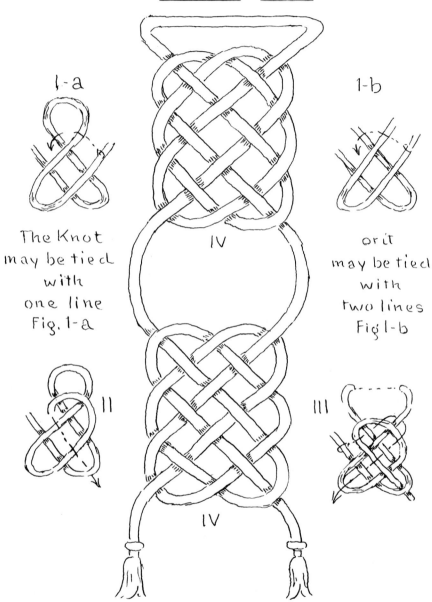

I-a

The Knot
may be tied
with
one line
Fig. 1-a

I-b

or it
may be tied
with
two lines
Fig 1-b

II

III

IV

IV

ADDING STRANDS to the CHINESE KNOT

I

II

V

VI

III

IV

DEVELOPMENT
of Interlacings of any number of strands

Fig. I
Clove Hitch
page 7

The <u>Bight</u> at A
(not the End)
builds up the Braid

By
pulling the 2 ends
of the line
the Braids fall apart

But
if the End of the line
(not the Bight) is passed
through the Braid
as in Fig. V
the Interlacing
cannot fall apart
and the work can be so ended
at any one of its stages.

TEMPLE ORNAMENTS

141
Details of Temple Ornaments

A – begins all four knots

B – belongs with Knots
I & II

A

C – belongs with Knots
III & IV

B

C

I   II   III   IV

I   II   III   IV

ORNAMENTAL FORMS
based on the
Overhand Knot

143
DOUBLE CARRICK

ORNAMENTAL KNOTS

145
CELTIC KNOTS

146

CELTIC
INTERLACINGS

Panels
II, III, IV & V
are modifications
of panel I

II

III

I

A

B

C

D

Fig. A
may be changed to B
or to

Fig. C
can be changed to D

IV

V

147

CELTIC KNOTS

148
JAPANESE KNOTS

1-a

1-b

I

See pages
20, 43

II-a

II-b

II

See pages
33; 43

149
JAPANESE CROWN KNOT

I

If the four
parts
A - B - C - D
of Fig. I
are crowned
Figs. II - IV

II

B   A

C   D

The
result will be

V

the
Japanese
Crown Knot. Fig V

III

B

D

A

C

IV

D

A   C

B

of which
the front and back
Figs. VI, VII

VI

VII

are respectively a square and a
cross

ANOTHER METHOD

III

I

IV

II

In the museum in Salem, Mass,
where many Japanese knots are shown,
this knot is labelled
the

SUCCESS KNOT

The square Fig. III
and
the cross Fig. IV,
when combined, Fig. V,
form the word.
KANAU
" The wish realized "

V

ANOTHER METHOD

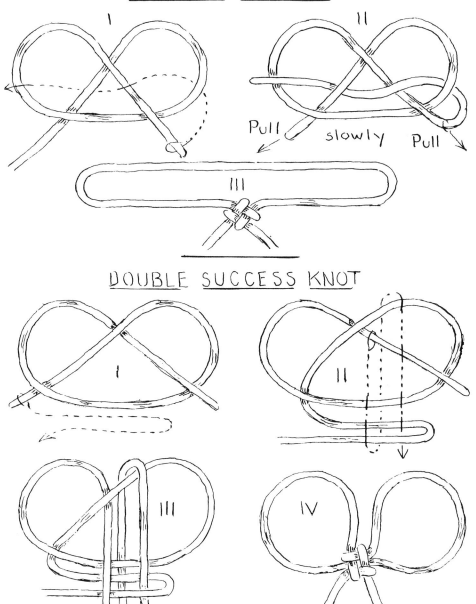

Pull   slowly   Pull

DOUBLE SUCCESS KNOT

JAPANESE KNOTS

153
JAPANESE
KNOTS

Lay the bight A
Fig. I
on the bight C
Fig. II

Interweave the
end-a-as
shown

154
JAPANESE KNOTS

I

II

III

155
<u>ORIENTAL</u> <u>KNOTS</u>
Suggesting the outline of Flowers and of Insects &c

156
BUTTERFLY

I

II

III

A B

A B
D C
F E
VI

A B
D C
IV

A B
D C
F E
V

The six loops
A - B - C - D - E - F
Fig. V
may be adjusted
to correspond with
Fig. VI

BUTTERFLY

Fig I-a

The Double-triangular Knot, page 171.
Its parts may be adjusted
to form Fig I-b

1-b   1-a

Fig. II-a

The Hexagonal Knot, page 176.
Its parts may also be adjusted
to form
a Butterfly Knot

II-a   II-b.

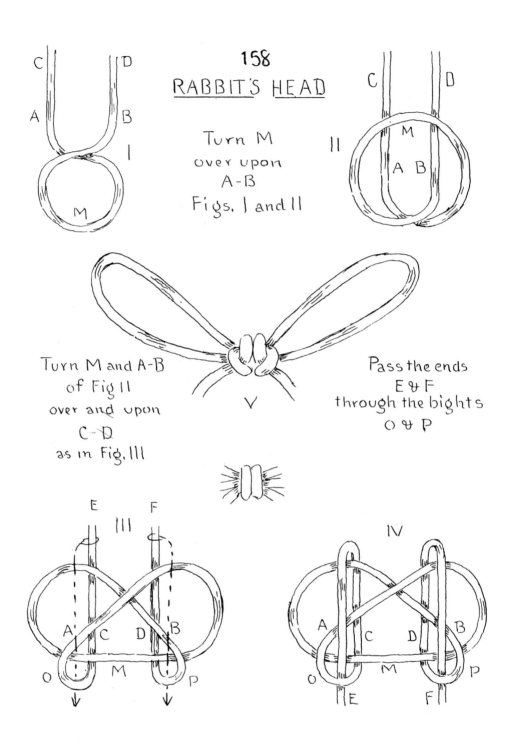

158
RABBIT'S HEAD

Turn M
over upon
A - B

Figs. I and II

Turn M and A-B
of Fig II
over and upon
C - D
as in Fig. III

Pass the ends
E & F
through the bights
O & P

THE DRAGON FLY

Figs. I, II. ___ ___ ___ Detail at X

Figs. III, IV
Detail at Y, Y.

INSECT

In the Museum in Salem Mass. are two Japanese Knots with the label "Insect"

I

One of them, Fig I, is a

three-strand Sennit, page 72 and probably represents an

III

EARTH WORM

The other, Fig. II, is a combination of two Macrame' Square Knots, see page 128, and may possibly represent a

BEETLE

II

Fig. II suggests a method for tying a

CATERPILLAR

IV

Fig. III is a series of Square Knots & spaces around two idle lines on which the knots are free to run, By sliding the Knots together, Fig. IV is the result

161

MODIFICATIONS
of the
Overhand Noose

I

II

III

The End
of the
running line

is passed
through
the Noose

TREFOIL

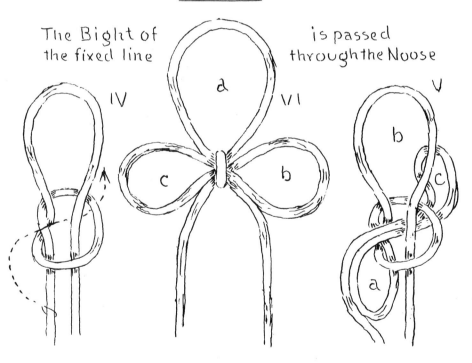

The Bight of
the fixed line

is passed
through the Noose

IV

VI

V

a

b

c

a

b

c

Fig. I — III
Flower from
a
Square Knot

Fig. IV–VI
Modification
of
Fig. III

Figs. IV & V
are the reverse
side

FLOWER KNOT

Fig. I
Position
of
the strands

II
Crowning
the
four parts

Fig. II

Another Method

V

Fig. III
Flower
of
three petals

Fig. IV
Reverse side
of
Fig. II

III

For Flowers
of
Seven & Eleven
petals
see
next two pages

IV

FLOWER KNOTS
of 7 petals

IV

Fig. IV
of
previous page

V

VIII

VI

VII

CHRYSANTHEMUM

of
eleven petals

Fig IV
of
previous page

V

VIII

VI

VII

FLOWER of 3 Petals

FLOWER of 5 Petals

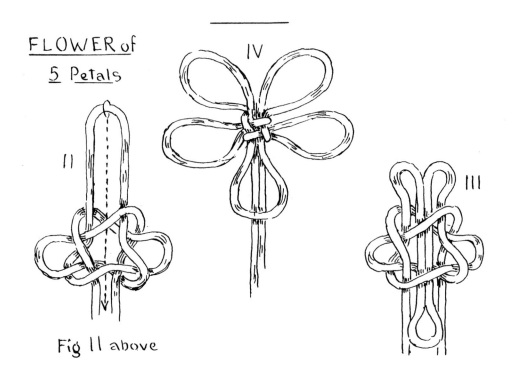

Fig II above

FLOWER
OF THE PLUM

FLOWER KNOT

Arrange the strands as shown in Fig. I

Crown the four parts, A,B,C,D Fig. II from right to left

A,B,C&D are again crowned from left to right Fig. III.

Fig. IV shows the lay of the strands on the back of the hand

To avoid confusion the under strands of Fig.III are omitted.

POLYGONAL KNOTS

These Knots are
probably
of Chinese origin
They may be tied with the aid of
pins
placed at the angles
of
a triangle, square, pentagon
or other regular
polygon

The radiating
strands
at the center of the knot
are double.
There is a top and bottom
layer
which are alike

170

TRIANGULAR KNOT

Front

Back

This Knot
may be tied on the
fingers of the
hand

Fig VII corresponds
with
Fig II above

171

DOUBLE
TRIANGULAR KNOT

Front

Back

3

2

4

1

5

6

III

1

2

3

4

5

6

1

II

SINGLE
QUADRANGULAR – KNOT

Figs. I, II
Detail of Fig. A
tied with
a single line

Figs III, IV
Detail of Fig B
tied with
two lines m & n

173
DOUBLE
QUADRANGULAR-KNOT

174
TRIPLE
QUADRANGULAR – KNOT

175

<u>DETAIL</u>

of the

Triple Quadrangular–Knot

The method is the same as that of the

single form

Figs. I, II, III and IV

<u>But with the loops in 3's</u>

I

II

III

IV

176
HEXAGONAL KNOT
Each Bight passes
through 2
Loops

I

II

III

IV

V

177

OCTAGONAL KNOT

where
each Bight passes
through 2
Loops

178

DECAGONAL KNOT

DODECAGONAL KNOT

DECAGONAL KNOT

Detail

Each Bight
passes
through 3 Loops

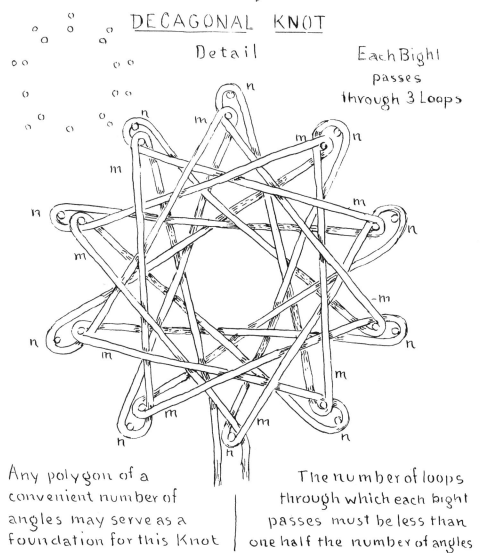

Any polygon of a
convenient number of
angles may serve as a
foundation for this Knot

The number of loops
through which each bight
passes must be less than
one half the number of angles

In adjusting the knot
release all the bights m,m,m, ---

pull gradually and equally all the bights n,n,n, ---

CHINESE TASSEL

181
DOUBLE INTERLACING

These knots (probably Chinese)
are based on the
Quadrangular Knot
page 172

I

II

Fig. I shows
the upper and lower
strands,
the lower strands shaded

The number of strands in each layer may vary from
two to four, six or any convenient
<u>even</u> number

In the process of tying the knot, elaborations may
be introduced in which the Carrick Bend
appears, pages 185, 186, 188

A
diagram
with pins, that
correspond
with the number
of strands,
is necessary, also
pins to hold the strands
in place as the work progresses

A
cork board
6 or 8
inches square
is convenient for
this
and other intricate
Knots

182

Two distinct layers
Upper & Lower,
the lower layer
shaded

B   A

<u>CHINESE</u>
<u>DOUBLE</u>
<u>BRAID</u>S

II

Fig. II
4 strands
wide

A

B

A

B

A

B

A

A

I

B

Fig. I
2 Strands
wide

III

The interlacings
are the
repetition of
Fig.IV

IV

Fig III
Six strands wide

A

B

183

DETAIL
OF
Fig II on opposite page

I

II

III

IV

V

A   B   A

B   A

B   A

B   A   B   A

B   A

CHINESE
KNOTS

Detail of strand A
in the knots
M

Detail of strands A & B
in the knots
M

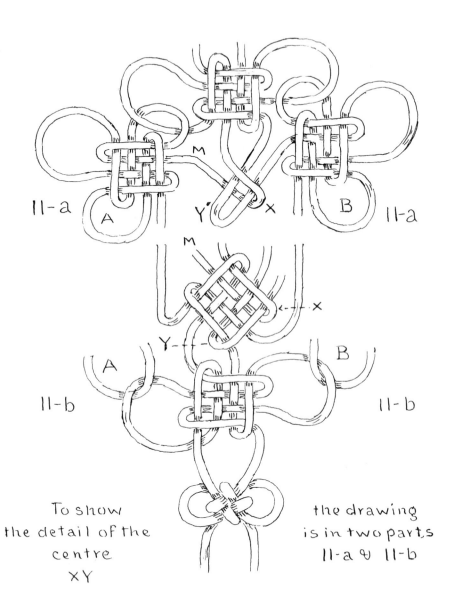

11-a   A   M   Y   X   B   11-a

M

11-b   A   Y   X   B   11-b

To show
the detail of the
centre
XY

the drawing
is in two parts
11-a & 11-b

188
CARRICK BEND
and
CHINESE DOUBLE BRAID
in combination
Fig. 1

CHINESE
KNOT
II

A

In Fig. II
the construction
of the
Knot at A
is
shown in the
Figs. III, IV

III

IV

TRICK KNOTS

Handcuff

Sheepshank

Man-of-War Sheepshank

190
A KNOT TIED WITH
ONE HAND

Fig I – Position of the line AB
Fig II – Seize the end A with the
little and third fingers
Fig III – Seize the end B between
the first and second fingers
and hold fast while the rest
of the line drops from the
hand.

191
<u>TRICK</u> <u>KNOTS</u>

The form
of the knot may
be varied
by adjusting the
parts

192
JURY KNOT

Loop B is placed
under loop A
Loop C is placed
under loop B
and over
loop A

Loop B is held in
place by a hook
while A & C
are pulled
into
position

TRICK KNOTS

String of
Overhand Knots

I

II

Pass A through
the loops.
Fig. II

III

Pull A slowly

Figure of Eight
String

Adapted from the
German